¶ THE FOOT OF THE RAINBOW

In *The Foot of the Rainbow*, Thomas R. Smith embraces and elaborates the hope for a better future, against the backdrop of turbulent times. His long-standing fascination with form leads to surprising, fertile juxtapositions of blues, ghazals, and Nerudean "elemental odes," reflecting not only the complexity of a multiracial America but a reverence for literary and artistic forebears as various as John Clare and Mississippi John Hurt.

D1446300

OTHER BOOKS BY THOMAS R. SMITH

POETRY

Waking Before Dawn 2007

Winter Hours 2005

The Dark Indigo Current 2000

Horse of Earth 1994

Keeping the Star 1988

CHAPBOOKS

Kinnickinnic 2008

Peace Vigil: Poems for an Election Year (and After) 2004

North Country 2001

The Lost Music 1996

EDITED VOLUMES

What Happened When He Went to the Store for Bread:
Poems by Alden Nowlan 1993

Walking Swiftly: Writings and Images on the Occasion
of Robert Bly's 65th Birthday 1992

Thomas R. Smith

Thomas R. Smith

The Foot of the Rainbow

RED DRAGONFLY PRESS
MINNESOTA
2010

ISBN 978-1-890193-21-8

Library of Congress Control Number: 2010926917

Grateful thanks to the editors of the following publications, in which many of these poems appeared, sometimes in earlier or variant versions: 5 AM, Alhambra Poetry Calendar 2010 (Belgium), Askew, The Bitter Oleander, Blueroad Reader, Cezanne's Carrot (online), Chrysalis Reader, Free Verse, Great River Review, Grey Sparrow, Loose Leaf (online), Mindscapes, New Verse News (online), Pemmican (online), Poetry East, Poetry Sky (online), Poiesis: A Journal of the Arts and Communication (Canada), Pudding, The Whistling Shade, Worcester Review.

"Unfinished" originally appeared in the chapbook, The Lost Music, Bookpress, 1996. "Peace" also appeared in a Chinese translation by Yuan Liang on the Poetry Sky web site. "Ode to the Vinyl Record" was reprinted in Milwaukee's Shepherd Express poetry web column edited by Susan Firer.

My gratitude to the editors who first published these poems, and especially to Scott King for believing in this book. Without his tireless efforts, poetry in the Midwest and in America would be much poorer. A gigantic thanks also to Perry Ingli for his dazzling original cover art. He is a contemporary Turner.

Designed and typeset by Scott King
using Quadraat & Quadraat Sans, a digital type by Fred Smeijers

Published by Red Dragonfly Press
307 Oxford Street
Northfield, MN 55057
www.reddragonflypress.org

—to Krista

a promise for the road ahead

CONTENTS

COMMITMENTS

To what is true in all religion. To never
      argue about God (what He wants or intends,
      whose side He's on, whether He's a He,
      She or It). In this we are truly blind,
      before an infinitely complex elephant.

To take the side of human happiness
      against the powers of disaster,
      plague and war. Marie-Louise von Franz
      defined as "demonic" identification
      with natural forces that don't care about us.

To kindness as a way in this world, against
      cruelty. A woman I know, in a near-
      death experience, saw clearly that of all
      our acts, only the kindnesses, large
      and small, matter in eternity.

To earthly language in writing, against
      the temptations of academic head-
      tripping, the image always preferable
      to the abstraction that may merely
      deepen the reader's disembodiment.

To the indigenous belief that people
      become wiser after death, including our
      most bigoted and violent ancestors.
      (Including us, who to our descendants
      are sure to appear bigoted and violent.)

To the heart's intelligence above
        other authority, including and
        especially the hucksters of Holy Writ.
        To resist ideological strong-arming.
        To suspect systems and trust life.

To now.

¶ THE WORLD WE LIVE IN

AFTERNOON AT A RESORT

Take for your material the given,
what's immediate, outside the cabin window,
the needlefall of jack pine, half-lush.
Take the sky radiant since this morning when the wind dropped,
and the lake's bolts of shimmering blue silk
(and the splendor of last night's waves pushing
sheet after sheet of gold in the moonlight).

Take the seizures of cicada song arcing
over and vanishing like invisible rainbows.
Take the stillness of heat in which you can
sometimes glimpse the wavering image of childhood.
Take, too, the deprivations of that childhood—
the lack of money and vacations, your parents'
sacrifices—make them a part of the picture.

No need to invent, or to control.
No need, in your dimness, to replicate
the sun—the real sun is already here,
shining in the pen's dark stream across the page.
Each moment is a shadow-box containing
some enigmatic scene. Between the bird's
nest and the toy spyglass, find your place.

SNOWMAN

Storm-downed branches rise again as uplifted
arms. His wardrobe's a lopsided straw hat
for summer yard work, a tie from the back
of the closet, unraveling cotton gloves.

His nose is a superannuated carrot
from the crisper. For eyes, I've thumbed black
walnut shells gnawed out by squirrels. Three more
in an up-turned arc make a friendly mouth.

Water notwithstanding, he's pure greeting.
Rough as he is, I feel for him a fondness
verging on pride, as though I were a boy
presenting a crayoned sketch to my mother.

Man of snow, your crooked gesture of un-
complicated welcome instills in me
an urge for weeping, though in the early
spring days ahead it will be your heart, not

mine, that dissolves in rain. Because you raise
my spirits, I feel an inward thaw, am not
the wintry person I was an hour ago,
as much now your creation as you are mine.

RAINBOW RIFT

For Krista

On clear days I've glimpsed them often,
circling the sun, but never like this—
ethereal prism cradled among clouds
in a wind-still sky over the highway.

It's like seeing from a boat, beneath dazzled
waves, a many-colored fish somehow
leapt to earth from the bays of heaven.
On this date thirty years ago we embarked

on our seasons together. The land around
us pulsates with summer. Above woods and fields
we've found hospitable to love, a watery
rainbow shimmers in a cloud rift,

as though a blessing for the road we've traveled,
as though a promise for the road before us.

DECEMBER IN CUENCA

A blue wool scarf, purchased at a dry goods
store, keeps my neck warm on our morning
hike up steep streets to the Casas Colgadas,
"hanging houses" built on the cliffs' edge
sheer above the Huécar River. From porches
of the Spanish modern art museum,
we can see La Mancha sprawled tawny and
lion-like in the thin, clear light. Nearby —
gift upon gift! — a cathedral with *two*
El Greco Christs. On a high rock ridge,
we picnic on bread, Manchego cheese,
red Rioja. Soon it will be time
for siesta, our *pension* cozy
with central heating. Our comings and goings
add footsteps to countless others before us
scalloping the wide wooden stairs to the second
story. The landlady has a smile for us
because she can see that we're newly married
and need no more than what's here to be happy.

CHRISTMAS IN NORTH LONDON

Provisional days: everything in motion,
        subject to change, dynamic
                fall of Empire. I reveled
in the rebel freedom of the squats,
        heated my room with an
                electric fire from a skip.
Working for a cleaning agency
        mornings, I tapped out stories
                in afternoon on a borrowed
typewriter and after dark
        partied with punks, New
                Wavers and Rastafarians.
At lunch I'd scrawl determinedly
        in my journal, groping
                toward some breakthrough
like a symbolist seizing
        the curtain of appearances
                to yank it aside.
Everyone else, too, it seemed
        trying to rage through
                to more authentic life . . .
One night I woke to Cockney
        shouting from the street, a man
                bawling over and over,
"NO FUN!" Another, I watched
        a real fire-eater perform
                on a crowded rooftop.
A Labor Party politician
        whose flat I cleaned
                tipped me a fifth

of good scotch. In the Tube,
             feverish, my throat
                     sandpaper, I cuddled
that bottle as if it were
             an infant, hugged it
                     home to the abandoned
tobacconist's where I
             nested on the third floor,
                     alone. Early evening
snow glittered the lit
             vegetable stand with
                     their earthen wares,
pale, brainy cauliflower,
             knobby shillelaghs of brussel
                     sprouts. The city
going heavenly peaceful,
             I hunkered in my
                     down bag,
reading an Aldiss novel from
             the Camden library, swigged
                     my scotch and dozed,
surfacing now and then to other-
             worldly silence on Fonthill
                     Road and the glowing
orange bar of the perhaps
             portentously single functioning
                     coil of my fire.

MY LIFE AND I

We are generous with each other,
though it's evident anything
I love instantly becomes his.
I never tire of his stories, which
I know for a fact are all true.
For his part, he listens
without ridiculing my hopes.
Where we meet is the moving balance-
line between memories and plans.
We make a complete circle, his
looping behind, my sweeping ahead.
How could I ever feel poor,
knowing the note of each moment
is backed by the gold
ingots of those decades
he is carrying for me safely
in a satchel under his heart?

FEELING OLD IN YOUR TWENTIES

In memoriam Gene Nolan

That retired teacher you saw puffing down
the icy street with his bags of groceries—
how did he become a stocking-capped
duffer you recognized only in passing?

Like a good Boy Scout, you offered to help,
and like a good Irishman, he refused,
threw back his head and guffawed,
eyes filmy, thin shoulders shaking.

You remembered nightmares in your
twenties, of aging two or three decades,
from which you'd awaken, heart pounding
but safe, relieved to be the age you were.

Some people feel old in their twenties,
their first grey hair a tombstone.
But time weakens their grip on the gold
coin of youth, which rolls away

one day, unnoticed. We have other
coins. Those dreams are for making us less
afraid of what we're already living,
and of our old teacher up ahead, laughing.

In a friend's house, I reacquaint myself with the "LIFE Special Edition for Young Readers." Copyright 1956—I was eight, just the right age for poring over Chesley Bonestell's paintings of the "wastes" of Mercury and the double star Beta Lyrae bound together by rings of crimson hydrogen. Almost every photo and painting, memorized in minute detail, now leads me into reverie these many years later. Imagine—the world we live in!

But is it? It's true that the trilobite fossil dozes on, and has not yet awakened. Cumulus clouds, composed of some of the same atoms as those in the photos, shake their electric fists at dry trees on stormy summer days.

But not a single one of the bass, squid, katydids, coyote, sea anemones, opossums, kangaroo rats, king snakes or caribou pictured in these pages is still alive. This book of dreams is also a book of the dead. Not quite the world we live in anymore, though one resembling it, a seed-world perhaps, from which the present world has grown. A world the book's authors hoped the child reading would feel a part of, and maybe a little because of them, he did.

RAIN AT THE HOLIDAY INN EXPRESS

Droplets on the window multiply to a steady patter, then pelting, then liquid slabs sliding sideways against the exterior wall of the motel. Thunder like some improportionate judgment.

Lightning exposes radiant contours of the snapping sheets of rain. Downspouts pour small cataracts against the horizontal grain of the storm.

We turn out the room lights and watch the dazzle buffeting the night screen, the drama of the wind over newly planted cornfields, thin green lines scribbled incoherent by swarming pencil-tips. Rain, velocity, and darkness blur the fast food oases, gas stations dangling the bait of freedom, the giant mouse in red lederhosen climbing the Cheese Chalet, signs along the highway reading THIS LAND AVAILABLE FOR DEVELOPMENT and FUTURE SITE OF RYAN'S FUNERAL HOME, that home that is not our home.

The slant rain overwhelms all of these, confuses them with a saving indeterminacy. Amid this violent conformity, certain particles, wet sparks, the reckless ones, somehow freer than the rest, move in other directions. . . .

THE DECISION GOES AGAINST ME AGAIN

I dreamt mossy banks hugged a clear
stream. A thatched cottage folded into jewel-
like hills under the sun in its fullness.

I'd been reading before sleep about
the ancient builders, the elegant faith
of their few simple tools. A bald, mustached

man in a leather apron loomed at the door,
greeted me in his language, "Gud hurok!"
and I stuttered in reply, overwhelmed

by his stature and radiant strength and health.
A woman in the cottage, his wife, offered
me a flan. All furnishings I noticed in

the summer-flooded rooms—carved table,
chairs, a glass lamp—were worthy of Morris.
Later I glimpsed the woman at a fair,

a grave look on her face: Lady of carousels,
painted cars, and fortune, she decided whether
I, a foreigner without a passport, could stay.

UNFINISHED

Nearing town on a narrowing dirt county
two-lane I neither knew nor trusted to be
the right road, I rounded a sharp curve
to behold a cemetery evenly covered
by spring grass, set emerald-like behind an iron
fence among the newly-turned fields.

I've neither seen it since—although I know
that country well—nor looked for it,
maybe because that day it meant,
in its abrupt presence, something not to be
questioned, slipping away again quickly
after my road found the main highway:

Not sinister, morbid, or threatening,
but oddly respectful, a filter
for our rage of earthly aspiration
and desire: Waiting, agreeing not to interfere,
to touch only our death and not our life,
that most holy and unfinished part of us.

DARKNESS IN THE REAR VIEW MIRROR

New snow dusts its veil over the freeway.
Moist air diffuses the surburban glow.
Windshield wipers flap their wings, flightless birds.
A semi studded with carnival bulbs
flashes quickly behind, then showboats past.

Comforting shadows return, the dashboard
dials brighten, the rear view mirror lays
its black bar across the field of vision.
Ahead of me, safely distant, tail-lights
lantern a faint reddish trail to follow.

I need the darkness around my shoulders
to tell me where I come from, a beacon
before me to tell me where I'm going,
as I may lead those coming after me.
I need the night to find the lights of home.

¶ WORDS AND MUSIC

THINKING OF RYOKAN IN JANUARY

1.

In my birth month, I lie under quilts reading
the eighteenth-century Japanese poet-
monk Ryokan, also known as "Great Fool." He lived
by begging in the villages. Children loved him,
and invited him into their games. Most
of his poems came down to us only because
his friends preserved them. He compiled no book.
"What's there to think about, what's the worry?"

2.

Sixty years old, and I'm still trying
to bend the world's ear. I left my monkish
life somewhere behind me in my twenties,
tea and sutras on a quiet side street.
That small red house is gone now, replaced
by a contemporary apartment building.
We would still benefit from Ryokan's
poems even if every word had been lost!

ODE TO THE VINYL RECORD

The needle lowers into the groove
and I'm home. It could be any record
I've lived with and loved a long time: Springsteen
or Rodrigo, Ray Charles or Emmylou
Harris: Not only the music, but
the whirlpool shimmering on the turntable
funneling blackly down into the ocean
of the ear—even the background
pops and hisses a worn record
wraps the music in, creaturely
imperfections so hospitable to our own.
Since those first Beatles and Stones LPs
plopped down spindles on record players
we opened like tiny suitcases at sweaty
junior high parties while parents were out,
how many nights I've pulled around
my desires a vinyl record's cloak
of flaws and found it a perfect fit,
the crackling unclarity and turbulence
of the country's lo-fi basement heart
madly spinning, making its big dark sound.

MISSISSIPPI JOHN HURT

Deliverance arrived inauspiciously,
a car with northern plates dusting up
the road from the Mississippi backwoods
crossroads called Avalon. Who could blame him
for being wary? What would a young white man
want with the wrinkled black tenant farmer

who'd recorded, a lifetime ago, a few clear
songs on a borrowed guitar? We imagine
him keeping in a curtained bedroom
closet copies of those brittle seventy-
eights which, in a world presuming him dead,
had grown legendary in his absence.

From that spring evening's encounter
on a dirt road, a dream bloomed late, a fame
he'd given up hoping for, while never
letting languish the melodic, metronomic
gift in his fingertips. His wife remarked of
that time, "By rights, you know, John went into

this when he ought've been coming out."
Possibly he died sooner for it, though
happy with a happiness learned best in
obscurity, which perhaps in those last
years, flying from concert to festival, grew
into joy greater than his heart could bear.

For this man so fatefully lifted from
his delta share, who'd not even learned
to drive a car, it must have seemed as though
an angel had come to raise him from his toil,
maybe the one he'd thought he glimpsed the first
time a crop-duster appeared over his fields.

JOHN CLARE AND THE RAIN

Northern spring woods somber with overcast.
Against the flattened sky and lake, hazy
overlap of greens. Rain is in the air.
I write at the cabin window, secure

as your willow warbler in its roadside
nest. Nests and rain recur in your poems,
a terrible vulnerability, obsessive
quest for refuge for bird and human.

You made a playmate of your watery
nemesis, sent a shepherd and his
girl dallying under a hay wagon
in a cloudburst, dry as well-loved children.

You were a friend to all creatures fleeing
a destructive hand, often a wanton
boy's, though it was Parliament's pen that signed
you into dispossession and madness.

Yet in the asylum, you kept writing,
more than twenty years after your Helpston
haunts, spoiled by Enclosure, ceased to shelter
the country life on which you depended.

Storms blew it all away. Yet on the page,
you still eat peas, juicy, fresh from the fields
and relish a shower, havened by a
hollow tree. In the harder rain of our

century, we can join you a moment
in that space of inner protection, rest
among your warm straw words, safe and snug as
the cowshed robin in its "pleasant bed."

POET LAUREATE

At dinner the host presents the visiting
laureate with a braid of Minnesota sweetgrass.
The poet lifts it to his long nose, sniffs,
and says, "You know, this smells a lot like
the fur between the pads of a dog's paws."
Guests at the table titter, but he's
serious, this man who told the newspaper
one of his favorite things is to "pile up
on the floor with dogs Howard and Alice."
He has also, in a poem, famously
greeted his mirrored face "good dog."
I'm secret kin, recalling the many
times I've lifted our cats' paws to my nose
to inhale the homely sweetness around the claws.

For Ted Kooser

EVERYDAY

Do you remember the confident lilt
of that Buddy Holly Top Forty hit,
"Everyday"? "Love like yours will surely
come my way." It was as though, resting in
the hope of love, the singer had somehow
proven love already present.

How perfectly, boarding the small plane in
winter, he kept faith with that coming love.
Living in fear of the end is not living.
When we agree to fly, as he did that day,
the song remains clear and open despite
what may lie scattered on the frozen field.

BREAKFAST IN GHENT

Mist still hovers over the spindly November fields as Robert and I drive onto the main street of Ghent, Minnesota and pull up in front of the M&M Cafe. The morning's mood so far has been minor key, the piercing, icicle-like dissonances of a Grieg piano piece. But when we step into the cafe, it's the sunburst of a Bach cantata. Or rather it is Bill Holm, the first and only customer to arrive before us, in his shirt with rolled-up sleeves and blue pinstripes, smoking a cigarette (surely not the first of the day). Technically, Bill is sitting, but there is something of the tall man's slouch in his posture, as if from any vantage he must peer downward from his tower of irrepressible spirits.

The walls of this place exude a soft glow whose source is neither the room's lighting nor the cheerfully patterned wallpaper. No, the M&M Cafe is irradiated by some other energy, perhaps the overheated molecules of the story Bill Holm is even now in the midst of telling his friends, the cafe owners Marian and Mark, and certainly by the improbably robust appearance of the deep pink face from which blue eyes identify small details, perhaps unnoticed by others but extraordinarily interesting, in nearly everything they see.

Bill holds forth on recent escapades in China: his bed full of scorpions, and furniture "just sticks," a roof leaking in twelve places; his collapse misdiagnosed as a serious heart attack in Hong Kong and eventually, back in Minneota, treated with aspirin, "the $1.99 Kresge's kind"; how, enraged for six weeks by the injustices of Chinese society, he figures his arteries just "constricted in sympathy" with a bound people.

Bill complains of still feeling worn down by his travel, though Robert observes that weight loss apparently isn't one of the symptoms. "I eat," Bill explains. "The mouth is open!" and he points comically to his open maw surrounded by whitening beard. His alleged brush with mortality seems not to have intimidated him, for he whips out another Merit, lights it, and exclaims that someone must preserve these incorrect habits lest the world become too boringly well-behaved. It's clear he views his vices as an endangered species, and himself as a kind of joyful bad habits preserve. It may be difficult for him to imagine life without them, but it is harder yet for us to imagine a world without Bill Holm.

PERFORMANCE

I've been enlisted to play in a
classical quartet at Carnegie Hall.
Flown to New York, dressed in tuxes,
we're fed caviar and hors d'oeuvres
and escorted through a luxurious
sprawling building of which I exclaim,
small-town boy that I still am inside,
"This place must be a mile long!"
It worries me that I'm supposed
to play violin, an instrument I know
practically nothing about, except that
it's tuned the same as the mandolin.
I haven't practiced, in fact haven't
yet seen the score for the music
on the program. In desperation,
I take up my violin for a last-ditch
attempt at rehearsal, but something's
wrong with it, it's gone soft, it's
become a kind of squid in my hands.
I manage to straighten it, wedge it
against my throat, and skreek out
a rough melody, better, actually,
than I'd expected. Who the hell
got me into this, I wonder.
A voice tells me that I must
put aside fear and thoughts of failure.
Authoritative, persuasive, the voice
says, *Be steady. Trust yourself.*
You can do this absolutely.

NEAR THE BLY FARM OUTSIDE MADISON, MINNESOTA

The thickening buds need one good rain
to leaf forth in the late April sun.
Already the willow groves are misting
yellow-green across the dusty fields.

The old farmhouse back among the trees
and sheds recedes into stillness. Where are
the ideas, the talk, and high spirits now?
They're not here anymore, they've gone on.

I watch two deer running beside the mile-
section dirt road, then a second pair
closely following. They move away from us,
the friendship of James Wright and Robert Bly.

The horizon here is so limitless
you can hear the wind of the End blowing.
Don't worry about those old ones, they're
all right, what they've accomplished is safe.

Find that other, silent legacy,
all the things they have not said. It waits
for us along the roads, glinting like
the Minnesota River at Montevideo.

A MONTH IN WINTER

for Bob Samarotto, 1933-2003

I.

That December evening after the peace march
last time I saw you, I noticed on your
work table a copy of Don Quixote
bookmarked midway through. We tilted at Bush,
toasted poetry, its sustaining madness.
Your Sicilian fire held back the cold.
You kept my glass filled with dark red wine,
and sent trout from your freezer home with me.

2.

By a northern lake on New Year's Day,
I set a drained wine glass down on the dawn-
shadowed counter. It tottered to the edge,
fell, and shattered. In a hotel bed in
San Francisco, your hand dropped to the floor.
Driving home, I fretted that something more
than a wine glass had broken. That evening
the answering machine blinked, red-eyed.

3.

Your ashes flew back from California
without you. Life drained you to the last drop,
then broke the vessel. In December
I'd thought your time stretched far and shining
as the river on an autumn afternoon.
Now I wonder if you made it to Quixote's
ending. In the winter dusk I see you
so clearly coming to the door with trout.

ODE TO PABLO NERUDA AND HIS ODAS ELEMENTALES

Don Pablo,
I've watched you
troll the lightless
trenches of grief,
an ocean-
bottom fish
all phosphorescent
lures and elastic
jaws to envelope
the swift prey
of thoughts and feelings
that swim under that
enormous gravity,
while at other times
you leap free,
prodigy of the sun,
a dolphin
on the frothy
crests of joy,
belonging
as much to air
as to water.
But
finally
I know
you're an
octopus, needing
that many limbs

to sweep
into the cavern
of your poem
the multitudinous
things of this world:
wheat, mirrors,
wristwatches, tomatoes,
blue socks, thunder
storms, dictionaries,
yellow flowers, salt,
nudes, entire cities.
Old cunning Neruda,
with your bulbous brow
packed with images
and your drooping eyes
that have squinted
for centuries
through the sea's green
ink bottle, you
pull the whole treasure-
frigate of earth
down in your maelstrom,
into your submarine
forest of odes
lit by pillars
of sunken daylight,
to sing in sorrow
and homecoming
among the bells and
carved figureheads,

calling us back,
voyage after voyage,
to irresistibly
and ecstatically
shipwreck
in the waves
of your music.

SOUTHERN MUSIC

for Geoff Donison

Driving south all night, the car
sinks through rainy Missouri towns
without stoplights, until dawn
seeps up from the flat corner
of Arkansas. The roads stretch
out past rail crossings, water
towers, mobile homes, the late
winter fields insufficiently
loved, lonely and wide open
as a song by Iris DeMent.

An old brick sun breaks
over Memphis, then puts
its shades back on at Graceland.
Are you running with me, Elvis?
Pine woods of Senatobia
shine with Sunday morning rain.
Grey cypress swamps flood
the shoulder. Passionate spirits
coil among drenched, snake-wrapped
roots, unconsummated, waiting.

Is that you, hell-hounded Robert
Johnson? Is that you, homesick,
tubercular Jimmie Rodgers?
Gratitude to the singers, black
and white, this blood-bought

land has wounded into beauty.
I do not call your name in vain,
John Hurt, Billie, Otis, Muddy—
and you Nevilles, Carters, and Williams:
Lucinda, Victoria, Hank.

At a neon service outpost
of the new generic poverty,
a wrinkled black woman selling
pecans calls me "sweetheart."
We are citizens of a possible
country the singers keep for us
in their songs. February sun splendors
through clouds on a blossoming hillside
maidenly as an old battlefield,
where a white horse is grazing.

¶ VILLAGERS

I live in an occupied country.
— William Stafford

A HOMEMADE WORLD

We all live in one, Huxley said.
Look around, and it's here,
individual as a signature.
How have you built your world?

Many people salvage bricks
from their childhood homes.
They nail the old framed
prejudices above the fireplace.

They can't see out their windows
because they've recycled the smoked
glass of fear. Even their
books keep out light.

If you build with only
the things you've made your own,
a friendliness toward living
warms you like a patchwork quilt.

If you build your world-house
with toxic cast-offs, there's some
poison everywhere you turn.
And if you build your country

with bombs and oil instead of
wheat and schools—you can't help it,
you'll just go on electing
Disaster as your president.

VILLAGERS

In places far from cities, villagers
share their meager supper of flatbread
and rice with a stranger, though some give
generously, some grudgingly. They sleep
on mud floors as snow falls in the mountains,
grateful to be allowed even such small
comfort. Life, with its wars, vendettas,
vigils, and sequesterings, holds to an
implacable clock of sky. Are we, whom they
envy for our cars, computers,
and movies, so different? We also
rise in boredom and hunger to the cold
yellow slash of sunrise. We also
keep our holy book in a box of darkness,
drift away on the smoke of our talk,
have no leader worthy of space on our wall.
We also, it seems, are not above torturing an enemy.
We also rot in cells, unseen
by a world that will never know us.
We also are an occupied country,
have paid with our children's blood
for tanks rusting beside the roads.
And we too are maddeningly capricious,
capable of cruelty or kindness toward strangers.

PEACE

White owl-feathers of snow brush the car,
hardly touching it. I think of friends
I haven't seen in years, flown out of reach,
in my mind never growing older.
Memory's fondness for things as we've known them
opens us to shock after shock. Only those
near at hand seem to travel at our speed,
ordinary diminishments barely
registering, until one day the sudden glance
in which we *see*. And what if, against the odds,
the body should prevail its brief span
to ripen naturally, without being blasted,
blown to bits, drowned, burned, crushed or
tortured, what then? Even so "peace" might hold
more than we can stand of sorrow.

THE GREAT PACIFIC GARBAGE PATCH

What are we, if not our dream of a better world?
Feudal times have returned to mock us, the names
of the new fiefdoms Halliburton and Exxon.

In the Pacific there's a floating mass of garbage
twice the size of Texas. (Google it.) It's spreading,
the first state of the country of the future.

When did we become a trash island filling
space between oceans? Was it when the foolish
actor's voice filled the space between our ears?

I felt so sad learning of Teddy Kennedy's
illness. In Nineteen-eighty he was ready to
set out on that higher road we might have taken.

We killed our King and dumped his wealth in the sea.
Our talk became wind keening through the mouth
of a plastic bottle washed up on the beach.

Thomas, you cried listening to Al Gore's concession
speech because it meant that the lovers in the song
really were going to die hiding on those back streets.

TWELVE AND TWELVE BLUES

January 3, 2006

Our white Christmas has dissolved
to a grey fog numbing the senses.
I walk in a shroud of war, searching for
the saving light of an opening. It's
giving me the brain-clouded blues, and I
wonder if I'll ever see the blue sky again.

★

Two hundred and sixty feet down
we felt the violence—earth moving
under, around, and above us. After
that shifting, silence, nothing over our
heads but a shocked, coal-starred darkness.
Twelve of us would never see the blue sky again.

★

We were all asleep in Beiji—
an "unmanned drone" came for insurgents
but found us. Fire and dust smothered our dreams.
They carried us—my mother, sisters, and
brothers—out in our nightclothes and blankets,
twelve of us who'll never see the blue sky again.

★

Twelve and twelve trouble my heart,
uncanny equivalence. How are we
to live so, without sun? Could we be
over now, the country itself hurtling like
an unmanned drone? Still hope raises my head:
How long until we will see the blue sky again?

STOPPING IN PESHTIGO, WISCONSIN, JULY 31, 2006

Mass grave: one of the most ominous
    phrases in the language.

Bombs continue to fall on southern
    Lebanon—I turn off the car radio.

We enter Peshtigo, by appearances
    just another town along the highway,

though here on October eighth,
    1871, the night of the great

Chicago fire, meteorites
    sparked the drought-dried woods

to flame. Autumn winds fanned
    the tinder-town to an inferno,

a thousand-degree tornado leaving
    not a single structure intact.

The Peshtigo Fire Museum dresses death
    up in its best blaze-orange robes.

One hundred and thirty-five years
    after those smoky bone-charred streets,

we pause before the fire cemetery's
    plain gray marker, MASS GRAVE,

where hundreds of the unidentified—
                unidentifiable—lie

together in a democracy
                under the skin, their agonies,

at least, put to rest, healed
                over, unlike that far-away suffering

the television screen brings
                nearer, new mass graves being

dug for whole families burned by
                our tax billions set afire, falling.

WINTER OF 2007

Many feel the cold now. Economists argue
whether we're in a recession, while our
national immune system lies down on the ice.

The most dangerous wind-chill is inside us.
Our heart is that man who fell down coming home
and was found the next morning frozen on the street.

The President sings that freedom really is "just another
word for nothing left to lose." The old soldier promises
to do anything necessary to defend the war.

A third of the signers of the Declaration were repaid
for their courage with ruin and death. What risk
in putting our names on poems to divert the privileged?

We fall asleep during the winter soldier's
testimony, and dream that a Black Prince will
slash through thorns, kill the dragon, and wake us.

Thomas, you woke earlier than some, later than others.
You still turn on public radio anxious for news
of Washington's ragged army camped in the snow.

OBAMA LISTENING

He has the look of a man who has just come
through a long winter, his eyes closed
and chin raised, in pleasantly warm sunlight,
He soaks it up and lets it sink into himself,
tries not to miss any intensity of the occasion.
Concentration gives his face not quite handsomeness
but instead a beauty that the Civil Rights veterans
in Selma might recognize, and the midnight
partygoers in Kenya, their faces shining,
and Lincoln, among his better angels, seriousness
of an old soul communing with the ancestors.
His chin-raised solemnity and absorption,
in which we can read both surrender and resolve,
remind me in ways I cannot fathom of the faces,
neither youthful nor black, of my own grandfathers.

Inauguration Day, January 20, 2009

A RITE OF SPRING

The Garden Club's plant sale at the Armory:
Faces, fresh and airy as the flats of
geraniums and zinnias, a partial
reply to the song by Pete Seeger, ninety
years old last week. Maybe someday,
at least a little because of him, the armories
of this world "gone to flowers every one."

For Pete Seeger

ODE TO SHADE

In my back yard,
two black walnut
trees converge
to roll down
their long
bolt of shade.
The fabric,
delicate,
lacy, lets pin-
wheeling mandalas
of daylight in
between the spirals
of leafleted stems.
They wave
a filigreed plume
in summer winds,
contributing coolness,
throwing leafy sprays
over the hammock's
delighted occupant.
Green
layered uprush
mountaining
cumulonimbus
towering storm
bringing
rain of shade
to the sweltering earth!

At the bottom
of its cool well,
we sit on lawn
chairs, modest,
low to the ground
as figures
in Chinese landscape
painting, humanity
properly scaled
to the great, slow
cataclysms of nature.
Is there anything
we do as perfectly
as the trees'
leafing? What
do we make
from the light we're given?
We blaze readily
into conflagrations,
terrible fires
that can never
be taken back.
Better to seek
refuge
from the winds
that stoke rage,
sheltered under
a great tree,
accumulator
of peace, holding

out to all in this
torched world
the hope of a place
at a calm table
like this one,
together in
the freely-offered,
freely-taken
shade.

DECADE BLUES

December 1ɔ, ꜱ00ɏ

After Solstice, they say, for a few days
the light doesn't grow any longer,
as if the sun were stuck in 'Low.'

Remember the relief we felt on New
Year's Day, 2000: no Y2K bug,
the road open before us, daylight-clear.

It didn't last. Living in America quickly
became like riding on a ship whose crew
denies the existence of the ocean.

There should be a word for the crime of killing
the chance for a fresh start that drew millions
to our shores. How about 'democracide'?

Maybe it's best if the sun stays down in
the eye of the needle for a few more nights.
Dreams need to be dreamt, and that takes darkness.

Let's not give up our hope for change, even
though in the new decade we glimpse others
on the Up escalator while we ride down.

KINNICKINNIC RIVER EAGLE

Second-to-last day of the year. Temperature
falling, harsh wind chafing our faces. Abruptly,
from the russet cover of oaks, an immense-
winged blackness breaks over the path, then lights
on a branch overhanging the frozen shore.
We recognize that blackness by the white
feathers scalloping its tail, the snow-white head.
And I remember: Our town has an eagle!

Up around the bend, a stretch of open water
the eagle must be watching for prey,
otherwise deserted by all but a handful
of die-hard geese foraging here and in
harvested fields, the big flocks flown south . . .
In a winter like this, it would be easy to
credit the doubters, when to all appearances
"the snows of yesteryear" have returned.

It's hard to wrap around how warming ocean
currents can give rise to blizzards locking in
the whole Pacific Northwest at Christmas.
Some say that by century's end, Wisconsin
could be hot and dry as Texas. What then
are the fates of river, trout, and eagle?
Head's work is to learn, heart's work to care.
Sometimes I forget: Our town has an eagle.

¶ THERE IS STILL TIME

ODE TO THANKS

If the only prayer you say in your life is thank you, that would suffice. — Meister Eckhart

I pronounce the word
Thanks, how
surprising and varied
its sounds!
Thanks, you begin
at the lips and teeth,
pull back
from the word-door,
execute a backwards
somersault off
the roof of the mouth,
and tumble easily
down the tongue
and out into air.

Released into the world,
your important
work begins,
laying down
your nasal vowel,
a plank upon which
we step
gracefully across
the chasm of discourtesy.

You're a skeleton
key that opens

unsuspected doors,
combination to a safe
full of hoarded
smiles, magic
word that reassembles
the scattered bones
of civility.
You're a spell
against the taken-
for-granted, a talisman
against the darkness
of the rude self.

Each time someone
acknowledges a gift,
you're present,
which is why,
when spoken sincerely,
you're the only
prayer we need
utter, a connector
not only of
human hearts
but a bridge
to the heart of God.

So I say thanks
to that sublimely
inspired one
who first nurtured

a green shoot
of praise out
of the pent-up
earth of inarticulation,
who first
in whatever language
vocalized *Thanks*,
that original genius
of gratitude
to whom
all following
after, not least
the poets, owe
their thanks
for the divine
gift of *Thanks*.

After Pablo Neruda

THE PERSEIDS

At 2 a.m., the August night striduluuc
with crickets, the universe an immense
black heartbeat and ours a small pulse
within it, I rise toward the larger life.
The Toyota, willing complicitor,
starts awake at the whisper of a key.
The moonless fields cold, the Milky Way
unfolds its star map above the back roads.
I spread a blanket on the still-warm hood.

A bright point rips the darkness, a cat's claw
on velvet. And subtler displays: Mars's
train approaching far in the east; diamond-
chaired Cassiopeia; the Swan embossed
on eternal summer. More meteors'
crisscrossing hello-goodbyes. What a bargain,
in exchange for a little more sleep I won't
miss when I'm dead, meeting these fiery
travelers who give everything to touch our sky.

THE FOOT OF THE RAINBOW

In the west the sky lifted her grey shawl,
and spring earth flashed green in the sunlight.
I drove south through rain, looked out
my streaming windshield at illuminated
farms framed as though in a painting.

At a crossroads I turned east: a rainbow
curved so high I had to hunch forward
over the wheel to glimpse its full arch
against the dark. Then out in a field I saw
its foot misting along a line of near trees

like a rainbow's ghost. It was that close,
moving with me, the arc I'd thought far as
mountains! We must carry our rainbows inside
us, nearer than we know, near as that traveler
I followed rainbow-footed back to my town.

THE FOSSIL

Two shell-halves, torqued a few degrees
out of alignment, sandwich a grey
mineral where living tissue once
swirled inside its lustrous room. Is our
time for knowing the world much more than that
brief stirring inside the shell? Should we

be worried? Should the bottomlessness
of the planet with its dark, impacted
layers stacked in geological vaults
trouble our souls? Things are not as they
appear, as this bluish-grey stone scalloped
and fissured on two sides is not a shell.

In my car, pierced by the oblique oboe
strains of Tobias Picker's "Old and Lost
Rivers," feeling sounds slant unobstructed
through my body, I'm grateful for music's
way of parting the veils inside matter.
How can the cold ground keep from singing?

HAND OF JESUS

I can't stop thinking about that mural
on 31st Street, of Jesus's
hand reaching out toward the world: great
pinkish fingers coming down from the sky,
palm open as if offering a handshake.

But what it really offers is the nail-
wound in the center of the palm, slitty
and rose-colored like a small vagina
nestled there in its fleshy hollow,
the saving femaleness of Jesus.

That wound never heals. That's why it's here,
floating above us in passing traffic,
so that maybe on our cross of war and lies,
we'll take a little of its suffering
to moisten our sorely dry, scabbed hearts.

In memory, Fr. Ed Beutner

BIRDHOUSE IN THE PINE TREE

The last evening of March, heavy snow.
We can't always see storms coming,
but sometimes get through because of a house
someone has hung from a broken branch,
its door turned away from the wind.

SCARAB

Late afternoon in the woods,
in the middle of the path—
bear shit, black, studded
with small berry-seeds,
over which I'd have stepped
without a thought, except
that it moved. I kneel

to see if I've seen right.
Again, the black turd
rocks from underneath.
No choice but to
pick up the stick
lying conveniently
close by, prog

the turd over—nor
am I disappointed
to find on the exposed underside
a most handsome iridescent
beetle, copper-bronze
so metallic that in sun-
light it appears molten.

Oh storied dung beetle,
ancient filth-eater,
friend in low places!
Likely you were laying

eggs on the netherside
of that excremental house-
to-be for your grub

nursery. Forgive me
for interrupting whatever
necessity requires
you to lodge under that
bituminous manna, sweet
with the superfluity of bear,
doing your part,

like those illustrious
scarabs before you,
to lead a shining
new generation
into world-light
out of the night-
soil of Egypt.

THE BEES

In mid-day heat,
sparks leap about
a hole in the grass.

Two-way mystery,
the dark descent
and the rising into light,

two directions
the imagination
travels at once.

Practicality
recommends
a brutal remedy—

boiling water
or sand-fill to quench
that bright dance,

swarming frenzy
as of bits torn
from the flesh of the sun.

But I will ignore—
and not for the first time—
impoverished utility,

and delight in the luminous
industry of that unseen
forge in earth,

womb of myths,
foundry of stories,
striking from summer

dawn to summer dusk
seeds of living
fire into the world.

LILAC

The lilac shoot
I spaded from
my mother's back yard
and transplanted here in
sandy soil a hundred
miles from its mother-
bush I think is
going to make it,
though the first night
its leaves hung curled
and despondent even
after the creek gushing
from the garden hose
bathed its woody thighs.
What were we thinking,
to believe that owning things
could compare with the satisfaction
of nurturing some small
life along toward its
glory and strength?
But everyone knows,
whether or not we
act on that knowledge,
the dark machinery
of coercion
working day and night. . . .
Friend,
take hold of your

life and heart:
There is still time
to stand up from
the torturer's table
and walk out
where the bee is
sipping her golden
hour in the grass,
where there remains,
even now, more sweetness
than we can imagine,
and where earth is,
this moment, taking
the thin hand
of the lilac root
and placing in its palm,
unseen in darkness,
purple coin
of a coming splendor.

BOY ON A PATH

Stepping over rough pools
on the limestone floor of the Glen,
I look up and see him
climbing in a trance of
concentration, steep, narrow
ledge above our careful
wending. I think he is
an Indian or a ghost, so
silently and effortlessly
he glides the contours
of that half-hidden path
I didn't know was there,
where I've never seen
anyone walk before.
About twelve years old,
short black hair, orange
T-shirt, tan shorts—
he obeys other laws
than those binding us
to this damp streambed.
He is upright
as a votive flame,
so focused he might be
walking the labyrinth
at Chartres.
Disappearing
above and behind
a massive overhang

of rock that makes
all of us below
feel earth's impossible
weight, he comes down
among bushes farther
upstream, crosses a jagged
falls we can't ascend
from our position.
As he deftly feels
his way down the cracked
face opposite, I see
he's maneuvered
all that hard trail
with his bare feet.
Sometimes he stops
a moment, bends
to examine—what?
Is he looking
for something?
He doesn't see us,
but holds to his own way
separated from ours
as if by miles.
His must be some
youthful project of knowing,
walking this strange
and beautiful world
more his own.
He must be on some
spiritual adventure,

hermetically
insulated from us,
an excursion
so richly private
there is room
inside it only
for one.

LITTLE DUCK ON THE RIVER

A small swimmer
hurried to cross
that quiet mirror.
It was dusk,
feeding time for wide
mouths below, snapping
beaks, tearing claws,
spiny fins,
and the unfledged duckling,
orphaned or separated
from its kin,
was alone,
searching for shelter
where it might sleep
guarded by spears
of yellow flag,
long huts
of grasses. When
it saw us watching
in the half-light, it
skimmed over the top
of the water on as-yet-
flightless wings,
bee-lining
to a marshy point
where the dark
overhang absorbed
its single star.

World so large
and deep, keeping
so much hidden!
That tiny traveler's
wake on the twilit
water trailed
inside us, into some
dark depth in us
not far
from home.

THE RETURN

Walking on the park road
early morning, summer solstice,
we came to a place in the still-
shaded cool where, looking
up a grassy hillside,
we could see, through a gap
in the trees, the rising sun.

Burning clear with all
heat and strength befitting
the day of its longest dominion,
the sun, boiling from that
high nest of foliage,
lit a silver swath
of sparkling, dew-bent

grasses all the way down
the drenched slope.
So brilliant was that carpet
of light the sun unrolled
down the hill to our feet,
we stopped where we were
and sat awhile in pure wonder.

And I remembered an old
secret promise, deemed

unwise to speak, though
who could deny it,
seeing these folk, humble
yet adorned, nodding together
on their way back to the sun?

And soon enough we got up
again and wandered on
into whatever we had to do
on that day, though not unchanged,
having accompanied a little distance
on the morning road of their return
those illuminated pilgrims.

Notes

Christmas in North London: This poem is set in the Finsbury Park neighborhood of Islington, North London, where I spent some fruitful, anarchic weeks in the early winter of 1977-78. Electric fire is a Britishism for "space heater." A skip is a dumpster.

The World We Live In: The series of articles that became *The World We Live In* appeared in *Life* magazine in the early fifties. I owned the "Special Edition for Young Readers" adapted by Jane Werner Watson from the text by the editorial staff of *Life* and Lincoln Barnett. I have since the writing of this poem obtained another copy of the fascinating old book, which I heartily recommend.

The Decision Goes Against Me Again: I wrote this poem after a lengthy study of Freemasonry, attempting to understand what my paternal grandparents, Harry and Winnie Smith, were really doing at all those lodge meetings back in Cornell, Wisconsin. My investigations generally elevated my opinion of the Masons, as reflected in the dream this poem records. Could that aproned man have been saying "Good *hew-rock*"? An apt stone-cutter's greeting as conveyed by the punning dream-mind.

Thinking of Ryokan in January: My source for this poem and its quote from Ryokan is Burton Watson's superb translation, *Ryokan, Zen-Monk Poet of Japan*, Columbia University Press. (Thanks, Jim Lenfestey.)

Mississippi John Hurt: Virtually resurrected from rural anonymity in 1963, Mississippi John Hurt enjoyed three years of glorious recognition by a new generation of folk musicians and listeners before dying at the age of 74.

John Clare and the Rain: One of the crucial events of the English poet John Clare's age—and one which he registered on a profoundly personal level—was the passage of the Enclosure Act by Parliament in 1809. In Clare's boyhood, the land surrounding a village such as his own Helpston typically functioned as a commons, open to all, no matter who held the deed. But the Enclosure Act allowed landowners to fence in their property, radically limiting access to countryside. For Clare, whose first love, long before poetry, was the land itself with all its trees, plants, birds, and animals, this was a catastrophe. With Enclosure came a more exploitative view of the land, bringing with it the destruction of many of the cherished natural features of Clare's childhood. No doubt Enclosure contributed to Clare's madness, for which he was institutionalized for much of the second half of his life. Even so, he left over 3,500 poems, many of which remain unpublished.

Breakfast in Ghent: The beloved Minnesota poet and writer Bill Holm left us too early at the age of 65 in February, 2009. As this memento of my first meeting with Bill in 1992 suggests, many were worried about losing him even then.

Near the Bly Farm Outside Madison, Minnesota: Written on the occasion of a bus trip to western Minnesota as a part of the symposium "Robert Bly in This World" sponsored by the University of Minnesota, April 2009.

Villagers: I wrote this poem after reading *The Places In Between* by Rory Stewart, Harcourt. The intrepid young Scotsman trekked across Afghanistan on foot in January, 2002, shortly after the unfortunately temporary fall of the Taliban. Besides being an utterly compelling travel narrative, *The Places In Between* is a revelatory look at conditions "on the ground" for ordinary people in Mideastern countries, one our leaders would be wise to heed.

The Great Pacific Garbage Patch: The Great Pacific Garbage Patch is one of several "gyres," i.e. areas where ocean currents have accumulated massive amounts of (usually plastic) particulate debris. The Great Pacific Garbage Patch was first noticed in 1997 but only now has begun to attract widespread public attention, in part through articles such as Kitt Doucette's "An Ocean of Plastic" in *Rolling Stone*, October 29, 2009.

Twelve and Twelve Blues: New Year, 2006, broke with two terrible events, the deaths of a dozen coal miners in an explosion at the Sago Mine in West Virginia and the deaths of a dozen civilians in a drone attack in Beiji, Iraq. All this against the backdrop of continuing war and the depressing Bush presidency seemed to me ingredients for a new kind of blues song, hence this idiosyncratic formal meditation on twelves.

Stopping in Peshtigo, Wisconsin, July 31, 2006: This poem resulted from happening upon a tragic landmark, once known to every Wisconsin school child, during a scalding summer heat wave while listening to news reports of the massive Israeli bombing of southern Lebanon.

Ode to Thanks: I based this poem, both in content and form, on Pablo Neruda's "Ode to Thanks" ("Oda a las Gracias") ably rendered by Ken Krabbenhoft in his *Ode to Opposites* collection of Neruda translations (Bulfinch Press). My ode takes off from but does not duplicate Neruda's, one of the graces of poetry being that, on most subjects, there is always something new to be said.

Hand of Jesus: The late Father Ed Beutner was a priest and Jesus Seminar scholar with a poet's soul, whose indelible presence cut a swath through these parts before vaulting on to the Great Beyond. He may not have endorsed the theology of this poem, but he admired it, and that's good enough for a dedication. For Ed's sake, as well as Management's, I fervently hope they have Bob Dylan records and Sobranie Black Russian cigarettes in heaven.

About the Author

Photo by Jens Gunelson

Thomas R. Smith is a respected poet, essayist, editor, and teacher. His work has appeared in numerous journals and anthologies in the U.S., Canada, and abroad. His poems were included in *Editor's Choice II* (The Spirit That Moves Us Press), a selection of the best of the American small press, and in *The Best American Poetry* 1999 (Scribner). Garrison Keillor has featured his poetry on his national public radio show *Writer's Almanac* and former US Poet Laureate Ted Kooser has selected his poems for his syndicated column, *American Life in Poetry*. He is author of five previous books of poems, *Keeping the Star* (New Rivers Press, 1988), *Horse of Earth* (Holy Cow! Press, 1994), *The Dark Indigo Current* (Holy Cow! Press, 2000), *Winter Hours* (Red Dragonfly Press, 2005), and *Waking Before Dawn* (Red Dragonfly Press, 2007).

His poetry criticism has appeared in the *Pioneer Press*, the *Minneapolis Star Tribune*, *Great River Review*, *Ruminator Review*, and other periodicals. He teaches poetry at the Loft Literary Center in Minneapolis. He regularly posts poems and essays on his web site at www.thomasrsmithpoet.com.

About the Artist

Fine artist Perry L. Ingli, a native of Wisconsin, lives in Minnesota and works and exhibits in his recently relocated studio in the Northrup King Building of Northeast Minneapolis, from which he travels to experience and create his synthesis of the landscapes and waterways of the midwestern biosphere. His artworks have been acquired for the collections of the Minnesota Historical Society, the Science Museum of Minnesota, and numerous corporate collections, as well as by many private collectors. For studio updates and current exhibition activities, see his website: www.ingliart.com